Grace
Always open
your mind up to
all the wonders of
the universe

The Zing

The Zing

The self-discovery guide to help you go from living life to loving the life you live

Ronald P. Villano
M.S., ASAC

Ron Villano, LLC

Published by Ron Villano, LLC
1650 Sycamore Avenue, Suite 39
Bohemia, NY 11716
631.758.8290

www. ronvillano.com

Editor: Judy D. Sherman

Cover Design: Ricardo Rodriguez
Illustrations: Judy D. Sherman

Library of Congress Control Number: 2006905595
ISBN: 0-9785877-4-X

**Dedicated in memory of my son
Michael Louis Villano.**

He taught me more about living life

than I ever imagined.

His guidance is powerful.

This book is a product of our journey.

I pray that *The Zing* reaches

out to you as much as

Michael has reached out to me.

Contents

Acknowledgments

This book is the product of the events which have shaped my life. These events were shaped by people and circumstances - all of which were brought into my life by God's will.

The most instrumental person during my journey was Beverly Barthman. She and John Gacek are the two brightest Light Bulbs in my life who helped me become aware of the depth of change I needed to work through. They carried my spirit when I wasn't strong. They saw me to the other side by helping me endure

೮ continued

my journey so I could learn its lesson and begin to live life with *The Zing*.

Sharing the good and bad events with my family and friends helped me to form my ideas. My parents, Peter and Elizabeth Villano were my greatest inspiration. My relationships with my children -- my son Ronald Villano, his daughter Taylor Paige, and wife Shannon M.; my daughter Jennie and son-in-law Brian Ferraioli, and their children Michael and Scarlett Rose; my son Michael Louis Villano; and my daughter Alexandra Villano -- became deeper and more meaningful because we learned to share our lives with each other. Together with my brother Lou Villano and sister-in-law Geri, my sister Mickie and brother-in-law Roy Vincent, my sister Elizabeth and brother-in-law Barry Benson, my sister Therese and brother-in-law JP Trapani; and special relationships with Linda Perla (and Kermit), Clarissa and Maxi, we all have learned about ourselves by living through life's Crossroads.

I was able to refine my ideas by applying them in my private practice. My sister, Therese Trapani, LCSW, AC helped me to establish the direction of my career. I would like to acknowledge Andrew Hararah, D.O.; Eduardo Yambo, M.D.; John Walsh, M.D.; Michael Torelli, M.D.; John Muratori, M.D.; Sheena Apun, M.D.; Thomas Shim, M.D; and James Pierce, D.C. I also thank Mary Ellen Romano, M.S., MAC Counselor. Their faith and belief in my ability and dedication helped me establish my practice by helping to create a two-way approach to mental health. Clara DeRosa helped my practice grow in new directions so I could find different ways to touch the lives of others. I look forward to our continued relationships.

The complex task of putting these ideas and thoughts into the words and illustrations in this book was accomplished by Judy Sherman. Our journeys coincided so precisely. Her creative mind connected so strongly that it is difficult to know where my words stopped and her re-writes began. She has given life to the ideas written down a few years ago by myself and Jeff Petersen.

We were all destined to share this moment together. Living life with *The Zing* will allow us to continue on to whatever is next.

Introduction

I was alone, in the moment, and it was perfect.

Introduction

SEVERAL DAYS AGO, I ASKED MY BROTHER, LOU, out to dinner. We went to an outdoor seafood restaurant that overlooks the bay. It was one of the last places we'd gone before he went back to Florida, and I thought it would be nice to go back there and catch up on old times. It was an amazing night. The food was perfect; the conversation plentiful. It was like we were introducing ourselves to memories that we'd remembered differently, though we'd both taken part in the events that shaped them. But the best part of the night was after dinner, after my brother had gotten into his car and drove to the airport. I was walking alone on the docks. The sky was a perfect sheet of moonless black and the twinkling of mast lights on the horizon were like stars clustered around the blue and red speckled coast of Long Island. The wind carried the music of a violinist from some restaurant along the bay. All throughout this time, the conversation with my brother lingered like wine on my lips. I was alone, in the moment, and it was perfect. I thought to myself, "Life doesn't get better than this."

What did it take for me to have such feelings of joy and peace? It was just another ordinary day. I went to work; I did my chores; I ran my errands — just like anybody else. But during that time at the bay, I honestly felt that I had an intangible one-up on almost everyone around me. I was simply myself, Ron Villano, walking on this little piece of Earth, taking it for what it was, making it mine, being in the moment – and loving it. It's so simple it sounds silly. But what would you give to feel that good? What would you do to feel that good?

People go to church for this feeling and, yes, that is part of it. Some seek council from mental health professionals. They also do unhealthy things such as smoking, and drugs or alcohol. Sadly, most do not find the peace they are seeking. Thinking about all that makes me even more grateful for my life and the countless blessings I have. But, trust me; a few years ago I never would have thought I could be this happy. And if you see any bit of yourself in this story, believe me, you can change your life and be this happy too.

The loss of my mother on October 5, 1996 brought sadness into my life like none I had ever felt before. As is the case with many people who lose the ones they love, my mother passed on before we could talk from the heart. I was also going through a divorce. These losses made me feel ashamed because I held my feelings inside with both my mother and my wife; and now it was too late. I felt worthless — I was a bad husband and a bad son.

For months and months I felt like I was being hollowed out with no one to talk to and nowhere to go. I prayed and prayed for God's help. I looked to others to help me learn to cope with these losses and persevere. It was hard to pinpoint exactly when I began to feel better. As time passed, I began to believe that the guidance I was praying for had indeed arrived. The bad times were over and life had returned.

What I didn't consider was despite the support of my friends and family, despite the renewed strength I had in God, and despite my beginning to feel whole again, things could get worse. And for me it happened without any warning.

I remember everything about that day. It was sunny and beautiful outside. Things in my life were on the right track. I'd just returned home from work. When I got inside, I saw my oldest son, Ronald, crying and banging on the counter. I asked, "What's wrong?"

My youngest son, Michael Louis Villano, was killed in a car accident on July 22, 1998. Upon hearing the news, I was devastated but painfully calm. It was like everything had stopped and the volume of the world was turned down. He was traveling on Sunrise Highway in Patchogue, NY. Witnesses said he was doing the speed limit. But somehow Michael lost control of his car and it slammed across the median, directly into an oncoming tractor-trailer. My son and the friend with him were killed instantly.

There isn't much more that can be said about that. Words cannot describe the pain of losing a child. And there are no answers to be had in the face of limitless questions. Why would God do this to Michael? How could this happen? Why can't I have my son back? Why wasn't it me? God please — can't you take me instead? For about four years I was numb to the world. I felt that I would never forget and never forgive anyone for anything done to me now or in the past. I couldn't work and couldn't sleep. I was falling apart — and couldn't care less.

Then on one unparticular night I kneeled down at my bed and prayed to God. I prayed for a long time that night, and asked him to give me the strength to change my life, to give me joy and a life worth living.

It didn't take long for me to understand His response. The very next day I started out in what I call the "Tunnel" and started to do the work of changing my life. I began to read the Bible, then other psychological and spiritual books to help me change the way I was thinking. I began reaching out and talking to people again. I made new friends and strengthened the bonds with my old ones. We prayed together, cried together, and supported each other through many hardships. I knew that these were the people that God had put in my path to help me walk my journey.

When you've been down this low, you don't instantly feel great. But anything was better than where I'd been, even if it was inconsistent. Some days I'd know right away that I was making progress. Other days would only bring a short-lived smile — my face being unfamiliar with such a reaction. It was not quick, and it was certainly not painless. But as my face slowly began to recognize its smile, I began to feel like myself again. However, this journey was different than my last one of years before. I was stronger and wiser and, most importantly, happier from within.

As time went on I came to understand why I was getting better. It's because of this that I wouldn't trade any of the pain or time it took for me to get to where I am today. Naturally, I would love to have just one more day with Michael but I know he wouldn't want that for me. He has given me the gift of life; he has given me *my* life back. Through this loss and subsequent journey, I realized I wasn't living the life I had to the fullest or with the right manner of thinking. He came down and touched me and those that I love and helped us all move on and live the way we were meant to live. We were meant to live with *The Zing*.

This way of life was an idea that I had several years before I'd lost Michael or my mother. I felt that it existed, but I couldn't understand why I wasn't living the life. *The Zing* is a joy in life that is two levels above passion. It is the highest sensation of happiness – when you live each day from moment to moment and let God handle the rest. There is no reason to try and control what you can't because nothing but unhappiness, disappointment, stress and loss of time can come from it. *The Zing* is not only a sensation; it is a philosophy of life. It is a way to conduct yourself so that you are aware of how you can live the healthiest and happiest of ways.

I was aware that this type of life existed. But I had to experience the loss… I had to submit myself to the work… and I had to endure my journey. It was only then that I learned that *The Zing* came from within me.

This book is one of the products of my journey. It is filled with some of the lessons I've learned through loss and laughter, through the books I've read and through conversations I've had with friends, family, and others. This was the blueprint for the happiness I have today, even when I didn't know that there was a plan for me. It is my hope and prayer that by reading and doing the practices in this book, you will be more self-aware than before, have a higher enjoyment and deeper appreciation of life and never stop learning on your journey.

Ron Villano
July 16, 2006

The Zing

A level of life that knows that change is always good.

1

The Zing

THERE MUST BE A REASON YOU PICKED THIS TITLE out of all the other books that are available. It could be that you are looking for something different in your life. Perhaps you simply want to enhance your level of living by seeking and following your inner voice – a voice that just said, "*The Zing* is what you should be learning about at this present moment of your journey."

Well, in either case, you are reading *The Zing* because you are supposed to be. And that is precisely what *The Zing* is all about – being able to experience everything that life has to bring you. Knowing that everything has a specific purpose and meaning which will lead you to the next moment. How you greet each of these moments will depend upon how you dealt with the last moment; and how you dealt with the last moment will determine how well the present moment's experience will be. You live life knowing that whatever you are doing is exactly what is supposed to be happening on your journey at that time, and there's nothing you could have done to change it. Once we understand that we only have control of the immediate choices and decisions we make and that we have no control of anything anyone else does, then we will start to realize the full power of living life with *The Zing*.

I realize that most people believe their lives and actions will have a direct impact on others. Most times we do things in the hope of affecting those around us. However, if we are trying to affect and influence others, aren't we really trying to manipulate them into our own point of view? In reality, we should only be living and doing for ourselves.

Imagine living life being only responsible for your-self and your actions. You no longer have to worry about other people's problems because they are not yours to solve. How they feel about you doesn't mat-ter because it's not your opinion, it's theirs. You accomplish what you want because you *want* to, not because you feel you *need* to.

However, this does not imply that you should live only to suit yourself. The difference between the self-seeking "only to benefit me" approach and the unselfish "I value me" outlook shows up in the degree to which you show and experience love. You need to begin to value, or love, yourself for who you really are and at the same time unconditionally love those around you, regardless of what they have done to you in the past or present. You start this process by look-ing inside and redefining who you are.

Most of what we call "our" values are not truly our own. We live life according to what other peo-ple have chosen for us. Our parents, our govern-ments, our schools and our religions (just to name a few) all offer strong ideas about living life. These beliefs and values should not be accepted blindly, but rather adopted after careful consideration. This means changing and questioning your views. Unfortunately, fearing change is a value that has been with most of us for a long time.

The good news is that all of us have the potential to be mobile. If you don't like what is happening, move yourself out of the situation. Many times it's hard to identify exactly what the problem is. Remaining in an uncomfortable situation is common. Years can often be spent trying to compensate for what we believe is lacking in life. Without spending the time to question your inner self, you may never identify exactly how these voids happen. You just try and fill them with external things.

Take, for example, a boy walking on the beach. He comes upon a hole in the sand. He decides that he wants to fill it up. So he grabs a bucket, goes down to the ocean, fills it up and dumps the water into the hole. The sand soaks up the water and the hole returns. So he goes back to the water, fills two buckets and dumps the water in. This time it stays filled longer, but eventually the water drains once again. We know the reality is that the sand will never hold water.

Such is adult life. People can spend their entire lives filling their buckets again and again. Get a house, get a bigger house. Get a car, get a bigger car. Have one relationship after another looking to other people to bring happiness. Each new item brings its own responsibilities and often increasing amounts of stress. How can you expect these external things to fill up inner voids when you don't know how and why the emptiness exists?

Right now, spend a few minutes and think of a time that you put yourself in a situation where you did something that took significant thought and effort to accomplish. What was your *real* motive? Ask yourself these key questions: Did I do it in order to:

1. Make me feel better about myself?

2. Impress someone (spouse, boss, friend, etc.)?

3. Meet a requirement (business report, school project, etc.)?

4. Accomplish something that brought joy, absent of any monetary compensation or motive for advancement?

5. Keep my life moving in a positive direction?

Take some time to review and process your thoughts. Your journey along *The Zing* Highway will begin here by tying the past to the present.

As you begin to become aware of your true motivations, you will start to understand more about yourself and at what level you are living your life. Are you living a life that is being controlled by situations and circumstances? Are you living a life which doesn't make you happy but you are afraid to change it because you think society will judge you? Are unsure about where your life is going but it simply feels workable? As long as your answers are truthful, they will be the right answers for you. Each response has a lesson within itself. By looking honestly to the past, you can begin to recognize who you are today. The way you were raised, the good and bad times, the choices and decisions – all lead you to where you are right now. The task at hand is to identify, understand, and manage these old behaviors. The investigation into these answers is your entrance ramp to *The Zing* Highway.

This book contains five Landmark chapters which will begin to help you recognize and start to change these old behaviors and begin to work toward a new way of life. Each chapter will guide you along. You start by defining exactly what some of the old values are and how they show up in everyday life. Once you learn how to identify these behaviors within yourself and your life now, you will learn ways of making some basic changes to the way you think and experience the moment. Becoming aware of what you want to change is only the first step. You need to learn how to recognize what you no longer want in your life in order to take action to prevent it from continuing to misguide your journey.

Each chapter concludes with a short journal exercise designed to apply a practical and concrete approach. Putting thoughts down on paper is extremely powerful. Often, we let thoughts roam about our minds without ever owning them. Good or bad, writing your thoughts down lets them out and provides you with the opportunity to read what you've been thinking. Remember – your journal is your own. It won't be graded; it won't be spell-checked. Why you write is more important than how you write. Whether you share it with others is entirely up to you. Once you see what's been on your mind, you can begin to uncover its true importance.

The trip along *The Zing* Highway has endless miles with all types of twists and turns. The good news is once you experience what *The Zing* is all about, you will greet each one of these Crossroads with a new and different approach. Following the destination to *The Zing* will lead you to the most exciting and most fulfilling life you could ever know.

Passion: complete love and commitment to whatever you are doing. *The Zing:* two levels above passion. It is a level which has not only a love and zest for living; but it is always introducing and preparing you for something new and exciting, no matter what life brings. *The Zing* is a level of living in which change is always good.

How far along in your search for a more rewarding life are you? If you have been traveling for a long time, then reading *The Zing* will open new and exciting venues designed to bring you to levels you knew were possible, but weren't sure how to reach. If you have not felt comfortable about your journey, then be honest with yourself and acknowledge that you would like to take a different road.

Think of this moment in your life as garage cleaning day. You know that there's a lot of stuff in the garage, piled all over the place. Many items were simply "thrown in to the garage" just to get them out of the way. It's hard to find the floor through all the clutter. So you take all of the things out, put them in the driveway, sweep the garage clean and start to put the stuff back. When you're done, you stand back and admire how good it looks, and how clean and neat it appears.

Consider for a moment exactly what you have really gained. It's basically the same stuff -- just in a different spot. You've gained, perhaps, a few inches. It may look nice, but wouldn't it be better if you gained a whole lot more?

Now, I'd like you to think of this task in another way. Imagine that your mind is the Garage. You have gathered so much emotional clutter throughout the years and stored it away. But how much of this is truly your own? This clutter makes it impossible for you to see a clear path out of the Garage. You need to check things over and get rid of all the "junk" which has stalled your life. This could mean that you will need to let go of what was once considered valuable but has now become "overwhelming…" or "burdensome…" or even "a waste of time." Once you've cleaned out your Garage you can experience the joy of refilling it yourself. Keep the same neat and tidy appearance with a lot more room. This time you will fill it only with the things that are going to make you happy. This time you fill the Garage with the things you really want and choose for yourself. Just imagine living your life *this* clutter free.

This is how you begin your journey to *The Zing*. You learn how to empty your life and begin to use only what you truly want — and need – to have. Nothing gets in without you knowing exactly what it is, precisely what it's worth, and why you need to own it in the first place. You will learn to fill your Garage with the things that are important to buy. So, let's go shopping!

The Dumpster

An entire lifetime's worth of garbage can get stuffed away.

2

The Dumpster

Drive around any apartment complex and you are bound to see dumpsters — big metal storage boxes with enormous hard-to-open lids. You never quite know how much a dumpster is filled until you take the cover off. Bit by bit, people come out and put their different little bags of trash inside — all those things they no longer want or need in their lives. Just when you think its capacity is reached, the bin gets compacted down and now there's room for more. And more. Until at some point, it has been compacted enough. The lid stays open and its contents start spilling over the top. It can become quite a mess unless someone comes to empty it out.

In a way, many of us are "emotional dumpsters." Just like a real dumpster, we are able to hold a lot of "garbage" — which could be anything from simply a bad day to bad memories, strong emotions to upsetting and unhealthy relationships. Many people are able to dump their garbage easily. But for others, a problem arises because they don't want to confront the difficulties and frustrations that are in their Dumpsters. Many are afraid of facing the outcome – living through the change. So these feelings are locked up, compacted way down in order to try and avoid getting rid of them. Once they are packed down, a Dumpster personality will often do anything and everything in order to avoid dealing with these issues.

Socially, Dumpsters spread themselves too thin; make too many engagements and too many promises. It becomes impossible to keep them all, but as long as they are doing other things, Dumpsters don't have to stop and take care of themselves. They are comforting themselves through their actions for others. They are constantly busy, always finding something else to do for others instead of doing some work for themselves.

They often take part in other people's problems. They are the "go-to" people. Many are expert problem solvers; except, of course, when the problems are their own. Whereas most people understand when they are being taken advantage of, the Dumpster actually *wants* to be used. This gives them something to work on which they don't personally own. Often, the situations of others will seem easy and solvable to the Dumpster in comparison to their own. Other times, a Dumpster will create larger problems out of smaller issues. Advice given but not heeded will frustrate this kind of problem solver because they are looking for a sense of accomplishment. In reality, if they were aware of their own problems, they could focus their attention on themselves. In a sense, Dumpsters feel a strong need to "rescue" people from their problems instead of truly helping others or themselves.

There is a huge difference between a rescuer and a

helper. A helper is a person who is truly able to offer guidance and assistance often by "shedding some light" onto the problem. Conversation should be a back and forth flow of ideas. A good problem solving relationship has two-way, conflict-free discussion. And the best helpers have the other's best interest in mind. Not only can a problem be solved, but there is always something to learn from the exchange. Dumpsters rarely exchange. They simply "take care of it…"

Dumpster personalities also give the appearance that their life is absolutely fine. "No worries" they often say – because all their issues are packed down and away. They don't want others to solve their issues because they see their role as a problem solver, not a problem maker. Picture an orderly, nicely polished desk, with pens in a jar and a neat stack of papers at the center. Everything looks to be in great shape, ready to be of use. But try opening one of the desk drawers to get out a stapler. It won't budge. Why? Because crammed inside are tons of old papers and memos. It is stuffed to the point that when you finally *do* get the drawer open, the whole desk moves a little, scraping the floor, with a flood of papers and pens falling all over the place. The owner of this desk wants you to see how great things look from the outside, but would be ashamed if you saw what was hidden below — embarrassed if you saw the real person behind the mask.

An entire lifetime's worth of garbage can get stuffed away. And a good Dumpster, by adulthood, will have a number of skillful calculated ways of working with this behavior. They may have even succeeded in making life bearable for a number of years, even decades. They keep up the appearance of that strong, steel storage box. They believe they are in control.

Eventually, the Dumpster reaches capacity. Things start to fall apart. One by one, those feelings, memories, and relationships will begin to be forced out – up and over the edges of the Dumpster and into the world of others. If this garbage has started to surface, it often happens at the worst time, in situations that leave the person feeling ashamed, guilty or embarrassed. The longer they run from these feelings, the more stubborn they become in refusing to deal with them. They begin to lose the control they once had. Everyday activities become an endless source of stress and anxiety. Tempers will grow shorter, complaints get louder and longer. Things that were once never a bother become major stumbling blocks. They begin to *fear* life more than *live* life.

❧

Starting to sound like a familiar landmark? Perhaps you see some of yourself in here, and perhaps you see others. Recognizing these traits in others will help you understand the Dumpster personality and help guide you down *The Zing* Highway. Take a moment to think about some of the important relationships in your life. Do you have a Dumpster connection with them? Perhaps you and this person have had years of confusion. You may feel that your relationship has been mostly one-sided. Or it's a relationship at wit's end. Those bad conversations, awkward moments, and harsh encounters could all stem from an overloaded, leaky Dumpster.

Many children will see their parents as Dumpsters, for example. In this necessary relationship, years can often be spent "at odds." Both sides require things of each other without really exploring and understanding the reasons behind the requests.

The relationship can become especially tense when the parent's Dumpster has started to overflow. Children can feel pushed aside when offers of help are declined because, as a Dumpster, the parent feels that everything is okay. If the child tries to get too close or tries to get something they are not willing to give, a Dumpster parent will often shut the relationship down. *Not because they don't love or don't care* – and this is critical to understand – but because they don't want their child to see their vulnerability. Wanting to protect their kids from their pain, a parent's fear is that the child will no longer love them for who they really are.

Perhaps you feel that you have been throwing your problems into a Dumpster. You can now see that their willingness to help is actually an attempt to avoid dealing with their own issues. They try to fix your problems from their own point of view. Take a look at your Dumpster relationship from the outside. If your connection with them is "rescue" based, then your relationship is really only one-sided. What can you really expect to get out of this type of relationship? Of course you may be able to let some of your negative energy out. But most times you will have ended up with no real solutions; only a lot of talk.

Recognize that strained relationships like these can stall your journey. By looking from the Dumpster's point of view, you can begin to discover ways to change how you work together. Seeing how this landmark affects your journey could also be one of the keys to why it hasn't been working in the first place. And, perhaps, by making renewed connections, you will begin to empty out your Dumpster a bit.

❧

If you recognize this landmark as your own, then you have taken a huge step to map out your way on *The Zing* Highway. Ask yourself these questions:

It takes courage, strength and stamina to unload all that garbage.

1. Are you the person that most people come to when they need to unload their problems?

2. Are you the person who enjoys having something to do most of the time and looks for things to do instead of taking the time to do nothing?

3. Do you spend too much time thinking?

4. Do you feel that other people's problems are simple?

5. Have you ever felt anxious or panicky and just could not put your finger on why you have these feelings?

6. Do you feel that you have taken on too many things and feel that things are a bit out of control?

You may feel stunned at the discovery that your Dumpster is not only full but has been packed down for years. It can also be a fearful time. Encountering old situations with fresh emotion is disquieting. You, and even your friends and family, may see your vulnerability for the first time. It is hard to know what to hold on to and what to let go. It is hard because sometimes we give and don't know that we should be holding back. It is hard because we all want to be liked and accepted for who we appear to be and appreciated, valued and respected for what we do. It is hard to open up the Dumpster lid because we tend to hold back when we should really learn how to let go.

It takes courage, strength, and stamina to unload all that garbage. After all – it takes a lot to fill a Dumpster. When considering the multitude of issues that would have to be dealt with, it is no wonder why many would rather keep filling and packing down all those painful feelings. Years in denial have "force-trained" many to have excellent problem-solving and multi-tasking skills. Imagine if these skills were used *after* the trash is gone. Dumpster personalities could be loaded with productive energy if they knew how to use their intelligence, fortitude and skills on their personal journey instead of on the journeys of others.

Sadly, most Dumpsters do not believe they deserve all the things God has offered to them. They have been so shut off from themselves that they have yet to find their own true identities. They do not believe that others could truly love them for who they are. They do not believe that they could love *themselves* for who they really are. Once their Dumpster has been emptied out, *The Zing* can begin to enter their lives.

☙

Everyone can benefit from cleaning out their Dumpster. One of the ways to do this is to first take a look at what is in there. For many, just realizing and acknowledging there are things packed away can take some time. Even if your Dumpster is only partially filled it could use some cleaning. There is no "right" amount of time to spend on the questions below. As a matter of fact, even if your trip on *The Zing* Highway is moving along, you may find yourself coming back to this landmark to take another look inside.

Identifying your problems will then direct your

efforts. As you begin to work forward, these issues will come out of your Dumpster and you will begin to co-exist with them. But this time they will be in your life because you own them; you bought them. You will recognize them when they come around again. You will begin to identify yourself in a new way. You will begin to live life rather than fear life.

The following journal activities will be helpful regardless of how you identify with the Dumpster personality. Take as much time as you want to consider your answers. A well thought out reply will guide you the most. Again, by writing down your thoughts, you have an opportunity to see what you have been thinking. Space is provided within the limits of this book, but if you want to really jump start your journey, consider transferring these questions to your own journal where you will have unlimited room to explore your thoughts.

Remember, the more honest your answers are, the more successful your journey on *The Zing* Highway will be. And when you clean out your mind, you also clean out your Dumpster. Now when was the last time you did that?

Describe an experience in your life that relates to a Dumpster. The experience does not need to be recent, just important enough to have had an effect on your life.

_____

_____

_____

_____

_____

_____

_____

_____

_____

_____

_____

_____

_____

_____

_____

_____

_____

Who has had a Dumpster effect on the way you view people? Or the way you view the world? Or the way people view you? These would be experiences where someone put their point of view into your head and that you eventually adopted and identified with. You may want to ask yourself, "Do I really feel that way, or am I just 'expected' to feel that way?"

_____

_____

_____

_____

_____

_____

_____

_____

_____

_____

_____

_____

_____

_____

Write down your thoughts about what type of person you feel you truly are. As life brings us along, we often lose touch with our individuality; Dumpsters are especially closed off from themselves. Taking some time to establish or reconfirm your own identity will give you a base upon which to guide your journey.

_____

_____

_____

_____

_____

_____

_____

_____

_____

_____

_____

_____

_____

The Battery

You have the power to keep or give your energy away.

3

The Battery

WE ARE BORN, WE LIVE, WE DIE; BUT NO MATTER what you believe, we continue to exist. We exist in the minds and souls of those we leave behind. We exist in spirit with our Creator. Even our bodies go on with new life — in plants, the breeze, the ocean. Everything — the earth, you, me — is connected by the energy of this universe.

It is a limitless source of power and production. It is present in everything we do; and it is always changing forms. We feel it as happiness when we do something good and sadness when things don't go as we had planned. It shows itself as destruction in war and as creation when a child in born. Like everything else in life, energy has its opposite energy and both are necessary for anything to exist.

For example, think of a time when you were really angry. In fact, think of the time when you were the angriest you had ever been. How did you express that anger? Did you scream or slam your fist on the table? Even now, just thinking about it, were you aware of your body reacting to that emotion? If you were really thinking of a particular moment, your heart probably began beating faster and the muscles in your limbs may have tightened. We do these things because we have so much energy (in this case, anger) that we can't contain it; we've reached our critical mass, so to speak, and we need to release it, so we explode by screaming and slamming our fists into a pillow. What happens when we do these things? We release it into the air or the pillow, where it goes into everything around us and continues outward. And with the release of this energy a space is cleared, bringing with it a greater sense of control and calm.

Whether we like it or not, the universe could not exist with just one type of energy. Where there is happiness, there must be sadness too. Where there is light, there must be dark. Where there is life, there must be death. And though this sounds bleak, if we think about it for a moment, we will realize it isn't. The Lebanese poet Kahlil Gibran rhetorically asks us "Is not the (f)lute that soothes your spirit the very wood that was hollowed with knives?" Pain and other forms of negative energy are unavoidable parts of happiness but we can turn sorrow into music if we know how. By having faith and confidence in yourself and those you love, and living with *The Zing* in your heart, you will be able to use all your energy to live life the way it was meant to be lived: ecstatically.

❧

The sun is the main source of energy for our solar system; it is a great example of what the energy in the universe can do. It keeps us warm, it provides us with light and it keeps us "centered" in more ways than one.

But too much exposure to the sun can be bad for you. It can be merely painful or the source of a lifetime of problems. In a way, the sun is a battery, always charged and always charging us. Our responsibility is to use its abundance wisely.

Like the sun, our heart is our main source of power. It gives us the spiritual energy to function. Our heart forms the link between each other and our Creator. Through it, we feel connected to ourselves, to others, and even to the world. It is these connections that give us our inner strength. Just like the energy from the sun, we need to use our own power wisely. Charged too much, we waste power. Charged too little, we lose power. Charged just right — we have the chance of living the type of life we always wanted.

Imagine a large truck using its battery to power up seven cars. The other cars hook their cables into this battery and they all begin to work. Now, the truck driver turns on the lights while the other cables are still hooked on. How would the headlights look? If you said dim, you're right. After all, there are a lot of cars in this energy relationship. The cables that are hooked into this battery are draining energy and now the truck driver needs this battery to work for him. The truck was once a source of power and strength and now it's losing energy. In order for the truck to be powerful again, its energy must be renewed. How can that be done? Unhook the cables that were allowed to attach to the battery so each car can now work independently of one another. The truck will begin to recharge and will grow stronger until, eventually, it reaches its full power.

Just like the truck battery was used to power other cars, Battery personalities want to share their power by helping others. They often help others first before helping themselves. However, when they need to do their own work, Batteries will often not have enough energy to solve their own problems. Their "lights" become dim, too. Why? The very power that they want to give to others is not replaced within themselves. Their own personal energy, just like the sun, has to be in proper balance in order to live life with full potential. Batteries need to spend the time re-energiz-ing their busy lives — and finding out why they allowed those cables to get hooked up in the first place.

A good Battery is always hard at work; only they are working hard and long on things for other people. They go out of their way to impress, often taking a simple task and making it into an involved project. As a result of always doing for others, Batteries live very fast-paced lives. As a result of all this activity, their lives are in constant motion. By the end of their day, they often feel worn out. Many times basic chores for these busy people are pushed aside, because all their time is spent elsewhere. They often wish for "more energy" to get things done. Their problems and issues remain because they haven't had enough energy to get them done.

Batteries are the types of helpers that nudge themselves into a project because it is hard for them to hear "No, thanks." They are leaders gone slightly off-center. The great poet Dante Alighieri said that there is no such thing as hate, just "love perverted." Their love has become misguided. In their opinion, they show their love for others by doing things for them. Many parents continue to do things for their adult children often because they believe it is a way to show their love. But a parent's love for a child is unconditional – it doesn't need to be proven, tested or "given away." Battery personalities often don't feel that they have the love within themselves, so they spend time and energy doing for others to prove their feelings.

Batteries feel that they are the best and only right person for the job. They tend to over-think and over-analyze a project and feel like there's always something more to do. They seem to be the type of person to take charge of anything that's going on. Their work is well thought out, and thoroughly fine tuned. In return for a "job (overly) well done," they receive praise and acknowledgment. Most Batteries will be very modest about their accomplishments. They see it as no big deal — even when they *have* made an enormous deal out of the project. So a Battery essentially looks for people to give them validation – a boost to their self-esteem. They look to please others instead of looking to do things to please themselves.

Batteries will do things in the hope that others will notice and accept them based upon what they *do*; not for who they are. Being out of touch with their own identities, they avoid dealing with hurt inner feelings by keeping themselves busy for others. Low self-esteem is particularly power draining. Many Batteries take things personally and assume the worst will happen. They aren't working with the present moment. They believe that things could always have been done better or that things were done better in the past. Time and energy are spent worrying about things that either haven't happened or have happened already. By identifying these power draining emotions and feelings, increasing their own self-love and becoming more aware of their own identity, Batteries can begin to use their energy more wisely.

Battery personalities allow, and often encourage, the problems of others to be attached to their lives. By taking on these problems at the expense of their own, they are not able to balance their energy. They feel more responsible for other people than they do for

themselves. Most times they look to others to increase their self-worth rather than looking to improve it on their own. What they are looking for from others is the very things they lack. The Battery power that they willingly share by helping others is actually draining their lives. Spiritually, our hearts are our main source of power. And Batteries feel that their hearts are in the right place. If they have the right energy balance, a properly charged Battery can be a very powerful person. Knowing how much power you want to keep and how much you can afford to give away will keep your journey on *The Zing* Highway moving under full power.

❧

If there are cables attached to our Batteries, how did they get there in the first place? From an early age we, as children, were expected to "do well." We were told to perform our best in school, at sports, and other activities. We also learned that one of the rewards for a job well done was the praise of our parents. But what happens when that becomes a child's only motivation? Unfortunately, as too often seen today, many school age students are fast becoming over-achievers. These "top performers" are constantly everywhere and in everything. When asked, many of these students say that they participate because they "are good at it." It becomes an easy way to get the validation they are looking for. But while they may indeed excel and succeed, the real question is "do they *choose* to do it?" Sure, they're good at baseball; but if they would really rather be in the marching band then they are truly not doing what they really want to do.

Have any of these childhood behaviors carried themselves into your adult life? Often we find ourselves doing things for reasons other than simply choosing to do them. The holidays are an example of good intentions gone off course. So much time and energy is spent during the season on cooking, having company over, and gift giving. Many call it "too commercial." Our Batteries become hooked into the "giving spirit" of the season and begin to work overtime. By the New Year, we've become drained. Wouldn't it be so much better to enjoy the holiday activities instead of feeling like they are chores? By giving to others because you *choose* to share, you free yourself of the guilt that often comes along with fulfilling obligations. Imagine having a house full of relatives because you want to share the spirit of the season instead of hosting them simply because "it's your turn."

Too many of us are surrounded by this type of negative, draining energy. We are locked into old habits, even when they have brought us nothing but sadness or disappointment. We do for others without understanding the real or true motive behind our actions. Where do these old habits come from? Everything we feel, everything we know, everything we think we know, comes from something in our past. Whether it was the environment we grew up in or a life altering experience, we need to step back and take a look at our lives. By taking inventory of what we have stored in our heads, we can take a fresh look at the values, beliefs and damaged spirit that may have been around for quite some time. Remember, we're cleaning your Garage. And once it has been cleaned out, put back only the values and beliefs that you truly *want* to own. We cannot be perfect nor have perfect lives; the important thing to have is the life that is perfect for you. I will say that again, not a perfect life, but a more perfect life. When we surround ourselves with this type of positive energy, we begin to live life with passion. We begin to live life with *The Zing*.

In order to continue to explore these Landmarks along *The Zing* Highway, we will require hard work, patience, and *unlearning*. The best way to start this is to begin to see ourselves objectively, without attachments to the past. Questioning beliefs and values will let us begin to see ourselves not as others see us, but as we see us. This will help us to learn about the type of person we really are and how we can begin to stop the energy which drains our lives. In order to realize our potential, to realize our own internal power, we have to have the grace and strength to be able to put things in their respective places. This helps us gain back an element of personal control which has probably been missing from our lives – the very power that a Battery wants to give to others. By regaining control of our own choices in our lives we can begin to unhook all the cables attached to our Batteries.

How many cables are attached to your Battery and how did they get there in the first place? Unhooking these cables is not easy. Making changes to the way you feel will help you to learn how to better manage your life. The first step consists of setting boundaries, which is probably a new concept to those that are not used to looking to themselves for power. These new boundaries start to form the foundation for having respect for oneself and, eventually, for others. You begin to feel that your time and energy are valuable. You empower yourself with the choice to keep or give your energy away on your own terms. Deciding to help others rather than rescue them becomes a conscious effort. Allowing cables to hook to your Battery becomes your choice.

Knowing how and why those cables are attached will help guide you toward living the type of life you want. As you journey along *The Zing* Highway, you begin to learn about yourself. You become more secure with your identity. If you are honest with yourself first, then you can begin to be honest with the other people in your life. You can begin to detach those cables without feeling guilty for doing what you really want to do. As you start to become aware of yourself, you begin to set up better ways to deal with the people in your life.

When you begin to learn new things about yourself, you begin to feel better about yourself. And once you are comfortable with your own identity, you begin to see the potential of your own power. Only your opinions matter. Only your beliefs matter. Other people's views are their own. Remember, someone else's opinions will always be a result of what they know about us as well as what they know about everything else (*their* life experiences, *their* environment, *their* values...). How you feel about yourself is the only thing that matters — it is the only thing that you *can* control. You begin to confront life with confidence rather than conflict, inconvenience, and obligation. Looking to others to boost your self-esteem by taking on projects will become as foreign a thought as you having all the answers to everyone's problems.

By knowing yourself and setting up boundaries in your relationships, your journey along *The Zing* Highway becomes cable-free. You have the power to make your own choices for your life. You have the power to do the unexpected and change old routines. You have the power to keep or give your energy away. When you choose what you want, you are able to keep your own Battery powerful while you help others. The other people and other things in your life aren't there to create or give you happiness; they are there simply to add to your life. The happiness you are looking for will come from *within* as *The Zing* begins to enter your heart.

Even if you don't feel like you are a Battery person, you can probably recall a Battery-related experience. Perhaps you have already started to identify some of the cables attached to your life. Think about it and then describe an experience which relates to this Landmark lifestyle.

_____

_____

_____

_____

_____

_____

_____

_____

_____

_____

_____

_____

_____

_____

_____

This chapter discussed taking a brand new look at everyday routines. You can begin to learn how to make better choices for your own life by increasing self-esteem, changing old beliefs and values, and establishing better boundaries. Take a few moments to consider how some of these tools could help your journey down *The Zing* Highway.

_____

_____

_____

_____

_____

_____

_____

_____

_____

_____

_____

_____

_____

_____

The Light Bulb

And when you are aware that it's getting dim, you can catch yourself before you wind up back in the dark.

4

The Light Bulb

IMAGINE A BRIGHT, BEAUTIFUL SUNNY DAY AT THE beach. The sun is high in the sky and the brightness is almost blinding. On a pole nearby is a light bulb, shining down onto the beach with 10,000 watts of light. Its brightness is overshadowed by the power of the sun. The light bulb isn't noticeable as long as the sun is shining. As the day goes on, and the sun begins to set, this light source starts to become noticeable. At first it is just a dim light surrounded by brightness. As the sun sets, its brightness becomes more essential. When the sun has gone down, this bulb becomes the only source of light. It still is as bright as it was during the day, but now you are aware that the light bulb has been there all along.

Are there people in your life who are as bright as this 10,000 watt bulb? You may not necessarily notice them when things are going well and you feel that your world is bright. But just like that sunset on the beach, you may have noticed just how bright their light can be when you were surrounded by darkness. Many times, these are the types of people who help you in ways you may not have imagined they would. They help you without intruding into your life; and they help you without letting you intrude into their lives. They do not rescue you from situations. They don't let you attach cables to their lives. Their presence at exactly the right time makes this relationship extraordinary and life changing. This type of person who truly helps you is a Light Bulb, a powerful Landmark along *The Zing* Highway.

The relationship you have with a Light Bulb often begins with a simple conversation. Many believe that

Light Bulbs are easier to talk to than family and friends. Both sides have to have some type of inner connection for the relationship to work together. Sometimes their help is for a short period of time – they come and touch your life at a certain moment for a certain reason. Other times, they create bonding friendships. Light Bulbs let you discover yourself in your own way, with their guidance and support. They don't judge, they don't lead you where you don't want to go. Many would say that the support from a Light Bulb personality brought them down a more spiritual path.

They use their inner brightness to shine on those whose journeys have gone down lost paths. The brightness of their Bulbs is a direct measure of their character; the more character, the higher their wattage. Many Light Bulbs are people who have gone through tremendous hardship in their own lives. Their efforts are always 100%.

Unlike Batteries, they aren't looking for someone to give their energy to; they are just there for you. They offer their support without any motive. Light Bulb personalities are the ultimate helpers — once you feel comfortable with their help you to begin to let go and let them show you another way. Your connection with them allows you to build trust. You begin to realize that there are greater things in life which have the ability to bring people in and out of your journey at just the right time. You let their light — and *The Zing* in their heart — into your life.

∝

How bright is your Light Bulb? Do you feel that you even *have* a Bulb? The good news is that we all have the potential to turn our Light Bulbs on. Full wattage, fluctuating power, or barely lit – all we need to do to begin to brighten our Bulbs is to become aware. Many begin to sense this type of awareness when their Light Bulbs are dim and things are not going well in their lives. Earlier Landmarks have helped us to begin questioning what we believe in and what we value. We begin to explore a new standard for living by first becoming aware of our own selves and how we can look at our selves differently and begin to live life with *The Zing*.

The world in which we live is filled with so much to do, so much to think about, and so many ways to compare ourselves. Unfortunately, from a very early age we are taught to live by standards set by others. Our parents and friends reinforce them; we learn from watching television or reading magazines; we observe by listening to music and going to the movies. As time goes on, these "old" values become identified as what we should expect from life. We are taught that we have to work hard (very hard) in order to get an ounce of happiness in our lives. Once we possess certain appropriate and expected objects, we — through the judging eyes of society — are then considered successful.

The reality is that trends are always changing. So we are always changing in order to get approval and acknowledgement from others. Unfortunately, many people take on these pursuits for vain and selfish reasons. The desire to fit in as well as the status attached to popular and exotic possessions come to dominate many of our motivations for personal and professional growth. The stress of falling out of line with mainstream ideas of beauty and status can be overwhelming to those who have not learned that the standards of some are not always right for everyone else.

This means that finding happiness will be as elusive as predicting the next trend. We look to have the right friends, go to the right clubs, attend the right schools, get the right job and get married to the right person and then have children. We worry about having these things. This worry leads to stress over obtaining them and fear that we will not get them or they may not always be there. Since we believe that we will *find* happiness by doing these things, we put all our energy and time into getting these things done. Wouldn't it be better to simply have happiness without all this work?

When we allow others to determine how and what we believe in, we experience a loss of our own power. This causes a reduction in our wattage. Our Light

Bulbs become dim. If we are constantly holding ourselves to the standards of others, how can we get in touch with living the lives we want?

The stress of pursuing all those things affects every aspect of our lives. It causes problems in all our relationships. More importantly it causes problems within us, within ourselves. Because we spend less time and energy on ourselves, our Light Bulbs become dimmer. Nothing is ever good enough because so many of us may not have questioned if what we wanted was actually necessary. Remember the boy on the beach trying to fill in a hole with water? When you live life looking for outside things to *bring* you happiness, you never quite fill up your emptiness. The things that many people think will make their lives complete — a spouse, children, a nice home – all require maintenance, attention and work. When we are working on the external things in our lives, we often can't find the right amount of time to take care of our selves. Identifying our needs first and working toward getting them is how we begin to brighten our Light Bulbs.

What this boils down to is making the distinction between needing something and wanting something. Identifying something as necessary because it will add quality without stress to your life is one good reason to allow it into your life. If you want something "just because…," you may want to take more time to consider your options. And this not only applies to material things; it also applies to relationships. For example, it's not good enough to be in a relationship with someone that "completes" you. Let's suppose your own 100 watt Bulb is only operating at 75 watts. In order for you to feel complete, you would look to your significant other to provide 25 watts from their 100 watt Bulb. But in order for everything to be okay, in order for both of you to be happy with full wattage, the other person would need to be operating at 125 watts. It's simply not realistic. Each person is only responsible for their half of their relationship. Each person in a relationship is only responsible for the brightness of their own Light Bulb. When someone expects to get more than they have to give, they are asking for trouble.

Children, friends, in-laws, credit card payments — these external things can easily become the focus or center of our lives when in fact *we* should always be the center of our lives. Others may look at you as selfish for doing what you want; but that is an important risk to take when learning to live your own life. There is an important difference between selfishness and self-esteem. Selfish people do what's best for them at the expense of others; no one else in the world matters. People with self-respect do what's right for them and do not sacrifice their goals or values for the standards of others; their beliefs and needs are their own, and no one else's. As discussed in the last chapter, a person with a good sense of worth recognizes external rewards as a bonus for the internal work they have done.

The key to increasing the brightness of your Light Bulb is to do your own work, choose exactly what you want in your life, and begin to use your energy for yourself. Clean out your Garage and own only those things – ideas, values, beliefs, relationships – that you truly want to own. This way you won't feel that you are "wasting time" on the things you really don't want to do but mistakenly feel that you have to do. You will find that you have more time in your life because you have eliminated the outside stress and management of the things you don't really need and no longer want.

When you begin to realize that all your time is yours, you also begin to see that happiness is possible no matter what you are doing. For example, most people look at doing the dishes or cleaning the house as a chore. That's not to say that these tasks are entertaining but they can present an opportunity for re-centering. If you are having a stressful day and you choose to keep going, view whatever you have to do as an opportunity to re-focus, not as a chore. You do not live your life to clean the house, so don't let cleaning control your time. We can make what we want of the time we experience. Having a bright approach to what you are doing and experiencing will determine the amount of happiness that can be taken from moment to moment.

Imagine how you would feel inside if your Bulb was working at full wattage.

No one has control over what will happen an hour from now or what is going to happen tomorrow. The only things we can truly control are our own thoughts, actions and choices at any one particular moment in time. For example, this present moment, the time you are taking to read this page, is all that there is right now. You cannot both read and think about something else. This means that if you are here, in the moment, you are not thinking about the issues and stresses which can dim your Light Bulb.

If you are here, now, it means that you can detach yourself from past problems or future predictions, even if it is for only a brief time. Why take time and energy from your present life by reflecting on past things that cannot be changed? Trying to control the future also drains your energy. Time and energy is wasted dealing with an outcome that may not even happen. Save your energy for the only thing you can control – dealing with the present. The more time you spend living in the moment, the more you realize that worrying about the past and future decreases your wattage. The better you feel about the present moment the better you will feel about the next moment, and the next. Staying centered and realizing that all time is your time will help you see that the purest happiness always comes from within. This is living life with *The Zing*.

✌

So, how can we judge just how much wattage we have? By knowing how we feel. Identifying what we truly want in our lives is the first step. This helps us to feel better about ourselves. When we are happier with ourselves, it makes it easier for us to do the things we need to do. And by living more in the moment of our lives, we begin to learn that there is no benefit to be received from worrying.

But what happens when we have identified changes that need to take place in our lives? Often the real challenge comes when we realize that in order to take the next step, we may have to face the fears connected with change.

Picture a boat going down a river. At the beginning of the trip, things are moving along smoothly. When something is in the way, like a tree branch, the boat can easily go around the obstacle. As it travels along, the river bottom gets rockier, the water flows faster, and the rapids pick up. The boat gets bumped around and it gets harder to steer; it may even get stuck. Sooner or later, the strength and power of the current forces the boat free. The water is no longer flowing against it, but flowing with the boat. Eventually, it reaches a calmer part of the river and continues on its way.

Our lives flow just like this river. Just like the boat, we are the ones floating along our journey. Guiding ourselves around the problems or obstacles in our lives is easy when the waters are calm. We tend to enjoy the ride, until it begins to get bumpy and rough. So, we tend to put our foot out to try and stop ourselves from moving forward. We may spend a lot of time and an enormous amount of energy fighting the current. But at some point, either as a result of our own decision or through the decisions of others, we begin to move. We move forward and experience the change. It's uncomfortable and filled with unpredictability. The change is no longer going around us, it is flowing with us. And when the current has settled, we discover that we did indeed make it through.

Keeping your foot up to fight change is perhaps the biggest waste of energy. It prevents you from moving forward down *The Zing* Highway. Being stuck in your life can drain the energy out of you before you are aware it is happening. What would you do if you had more power in your life? Imagine how you would feel inside if your Bulb was working at full wattage. Being aware brings your life into your consciousness. You can prioritize; make better choices; and be happy because you are no longer going against what you either fear or don't want in your life. All the negative energy — all the things that were preventing your Bulb from lighting fully – will start to drain away. If you are doing what makes you happy, your Light Bulb will always shine with its full potential. Your Light Bulb becomes the barometer for your life – you can begin to feel when it is bright and when it's starting to dim. And when you are aware that it's getting dim, you can catch yourself before you wind up back in the dark.

Experiencing hardship and dark times in our lives gives us the best opportunities to learn about ourselves. When we learn about ourselves, we make our Light Bulbs brighter. It gives us a foundation to build upon when we are faced with a similar issue in the future. We know that if we made it through once, it is familiar; we could do it again. Only this time we draw upon our experience to help guide us through. The best news is that you rarely have to repeat a part of your journey if you have done the right amount of inner-work. When faced with adversity, it will take you less time to recover because your own Light Bulb will guide you from within.

Knowing yourself and what you really need and truly want helps to remove stress and worry from your life. Accepting change is what living in the moment is all about. By not spending time thinking about the future or the past, you begin to notice that the only thing that you can control is the present moment that you are in. Letting go and moving forward through the change, and through the fear of change, gives you the opportunity to learn extraordinary lessons about yourself. And while the purest happiness always comes from within, that is not the only thing which you can find inside. What you have learned and what you experience is what combines within yourself as wisdom. Wisdom and happiness — your inner spirit — is what powers your Light Bulb and brightens your journey along *The Zing* Highway.

Who in your life is a Light Bulb? How have they helped you on your journey? Are you a Light Bulb for someone else? How have you helped them on their journey?

_____

_____

_____

_____

_____

_____

_____

_____

_____

_____

_____

_____

_____

_____

_____

_____

What old values, issues, beliefs and relationships are holding you back from increasing the wattage in your Light Bulb?

_____

_____

_____

_____

_____

_____

_____

_____

_____

_____

_____

_____

_____

_____

_____

_____

_____

Think about a time that you went through a change. It does not have to be a big change, just one that impacted your life in some way. What did you learn about yourself as a result of going through the situation? How did you feel once it was complete?

_____

_____

_____

_____

_____

_____

_____

_____

_____

_____

_____

_____

_____

_____

The Crossroads

People can spend lifetimes waiting for just that one thing to happen.

5

The Crossroads

"We never keep to the present. We recall the past; we anticipate the future as if we found it too slow in coming and were trying to hurry it up, or we recall the past as if to stay its too rapid flight. We are so unwise that we wander about in times that do not belong to us, and do not think of the only one that does; so vain that we dream of times that are not and blindly flee the only one that is. The fact is that the present usually hurts. We thrust it out of sight when it distresses us, and if we find it enjoyable, we are sorry to see it slip away. We try to give it the support of the future, and think how we are going to arrange things over which we have no control for a time we can never be sure of reaching.

"Let each of us examine his thoughts; he will find them wholly concerned with the past or the future. We almost never think of the present, and if we do think of it, it is only to see what light it throws on our plans for the future. The present is never our end. The past and the present are our means, the future alone our end. Thus we never actually live, but hope to live, and since we are always planning how to be happy, it is inevitable that we should never be so…"

Blaise Pascal
17th century French philosopher,
mathematician, and physicist

Most people feel that when change happens in their lives, it's an interruption to what they have been doing. John Lennon was quoted as saying, "Life is what happens to you when you are making other plans." Making plans is important, but counting on them to fall *exactly* in line can create problems. The only time that change and expectations can go together is when you live life expecting change. Knowing that plans change, the best plans you can make are only based upon the moment. If we live in the here and now, life will not be just what happens when we're making other plans because our *only* plans would be to live life.   A better way to think would be to say, "*Change* is what happens when you are making other plans." Replacing this one word transforms the whole meaning of the cliché and helps you to begin to see change as a necessary part of living life with *The Zing*.

Change is a necessary part of living. Change happens. And if you are considering making an important change in your life, know that you have already lived life with change. Many of us use planners to lay out the course of our day.   Elaborate electronic devices or simple notes on a calendar tell us where to be and at what time. Then, plans change — someone cancels a meeting, or the car won't start, or the kids get sick. You couldn't predict that something else was going to happen, but it did. So, you adjust the plans of the day. Move the doctor appointment; reschedule lunch – whatever you need to do to make it work. Making it work means that you go back to living your life. But what you actually have done is continued to live life but with a change.

Along with the landmarks we have encountered (the Garage, the Dumpster, the Battery), our trip along *The Zing* Highway is filled with endless miles of twists and turns. These are points along our travels where we need to make a choice on which way to go. Most of us can look back and see how certain decisions have brought us to where we are today. But then there comes a point in our lives where we sense that something isn't quite right — that we have lost some of the happiness we once had. We begin to take a different look at our journey and start to see some of the paths leading in new directions. We find ourselves at a Crossroad – a defining point of our lives where we need to make a major life decision.

Young children are often asked what they would like to be when they grow up. Their answer usually relates to what is going on in their life at that time. We often lose this sense of "going with the flow" as we get older. As the stakes get higher, the plans become more involved and more difficult to undo. As adults we come to value our goals and the hard work we put into them in order to make our dreams become reality. Somewhere along the line, these goals have become the hopes to which we attach our futures. Hopes like finding "the perfect" mate, getting married, buying a house — all become a way to measure our success. Checking off each part of the plan makes us feel like we have done something successful. And when we are living within these guidelines, we feel that the situation is in control and we are comfortable.

However, the true reality is that over the course of time, even the best plans may need to change. Goals which may have been set awhile ago may no longer seem reasonable. What was once thought of as a "fact of life" may no longer apply. Questioning your own beliefs can be uncomfortable; and changing our course of action will often make us feel fearful and anxious. As a result, we often fail to take the Crossroad and use excuses for continuing down the wrong path.

Take, for example, someone working at a job that has become a problem in their lives. Perhaps the job wasn't what they had expected it to be or the management changed. In any case, they will often complain that they just don't like what they are doing anymore. However, many of these people will remain at the job. They offer logical explanations for staying, when in reality these reasons are just excuses for not wanting to face change. Yes, it may be tough, both mentally and financially, to change jobs. But when it really comes down to it, they are putting a very high price on their own happiness.

Getting stuck at a Crossroad also wastes an enormous amount of time. Time is spent thinking about problems and worrying about how they will turn out instead of doing something about them. Time is wasted because we are reluctant to change the negative behavior and impulses in our lives because we are too scared to believe that things will or could ever get

better. Time becomes a weapon that we use to sabo-
tage ourselves. We begin to convince ourselves that
things can't change until something *else* does. Do
some of these responses sound familiar?

> "I can't be happy until I pay all my bills."

> "I can't quit this job until I have another. I
> can't interview because I can't take time off
> from this job."

> "Someone has just broken up with me *again*.
> How can I possibly be happy with myself if
> nobody else wants to love me?"

We often spend time going around and around in
our head with these thoughts, making no progress
at all in solving the problem. Many of us have
heard or even given similar types of answers for
problems in our lives not realizing that they are
really only excuses to avoid change. Happiness
becomes conditional. Happiness depends upon

some outside thing to happen. Tragically, people can spend lifetimes waiting just for that one thing to happen. Time sabotages happiness.

Why would someone who is reeling from the pain of divorce *not* want to change? Why would someone barely getting by on two jobs *not* want to change? These are generally the people who want and need to take a new Crossroad now more then ever. But when one has tunnel vision, change is a word as mysterious and inexplicable as happiness.

ଔ

Consider planting a seed right out of the packet into the ground in your yard. You may have success, if you're lucky. But most times, the seeds never reach their full potential because they are often planted in the wrong type of soil. If the ground is made up of more sand than dirt, for example, the seedling may not grow well, or it may not even grow at all. But once the soil has the proper nutrients, it will be a great place to grow a new plant.

Each of us plants many "seeds" during our lives. This is particularly true at the new year. Resolutions – agreements we make with ourselves to change – are often placed aside by the end of the month. Why? Because we planted this seed in sand instead of putting it in soil. Faith, love, and trust needs to be nurtured from within in order to make any lasting change to our lives. Without changing the surroundings we are living in, these new (or renewed) goals won't have the proper place to grow.

While we often like to think that we are planting seeds, many times we really want to plant full grown trees. Besides learning to face the anxiety and fear of change, we often grow tired of doing the work. Patience is another hard lesson to learn when approaching a Crossroad in your life. A good amount of the fear would be eliminated if we could predict exactly how long it will take. Changing one's life would simply become a matter of will-power. You would just have to endure the change only; and then just move on. You become skilled at just getting by and coping with life. Experiencing the loss and submitting yourself to the work in the face of personal crisis is the only way you will gain invaluable and life changing insight and wisdom. By enduring the journey, instead of simply coping with the change, you reach inside and begin to tap into the power of *The Zing* that you have within yourself.

Do you feel that something is in the air? Becoming aware that change has to happen is like watching a tree change after summertime. At first, the leaves are still green, but the weather is starting to get cooler. You may not notice that the leaves have lost their shine and look a bit wilted; but they are still green. Slowly, the leaves begin to change and the whole tree takes on a new color. Then the leaves start to fall. Just a few at first, followed by many more, until there's just that one hanging by a stem. Waiting for the right moment to let go. Once this last leaf is gone, the tree appears different. It has gone through its change of season and now is ready to go through the tough, cold weather. And while the tree may indeed look different, it is still the same tree. It's firmly planted roots will stand the test of winter. In order for the tree to bloom again, it has to go through the change of season.

It's not hard to see that change in our lives affects us just like this change of season. Many times, it begins very slowly with only slight awareness that it is even happening. Once we begin to understand that something is indeed different, the true fall colors begin to show. Letting go is the hardest part and is what people fear most. When something goes away we are left with an empty feeling. It feels a bit darker and colder, until one day we realize that the life we once had has changed. But just like the roots of this tree, we have not changed *who* we are. What is different is the *how*. How we handle what life brings our way is what changes. We begin to be aware of the season. Our faith increases, and we begin to believe that the next season will, eventually, begin. It is with this faith that we can begin to accept that change is always happening. When you come to expect change and begin to live with change, you no longer fear taking the Crossroad.

We often look at our problems as a whole instead of as a sum of its parts. It's no wonder we fear taking a new path. It is important to consider breaking any problem down into simpler steps. This way, each stride you take toward making change is just as important as the entire journey itself. Whenever you hit a milestone, you may have an opportunity to take a look at your progress. By breaking down change into smaller, easier-to-handle steps, you can focus 100% of your attention on solving each part of the problem. Your best efforts produce the best results. Each time you solve a portion of the problem, you take another step forward. You gain confidence; you become familiar with working through change by tackling the simpler tasks. And you can take a look back and see that progress has indeed happened, and you are beginning to live life with change.

As you begin to live life with change, you are learning to live life closer to the moment. The huge problem that you were once facing has become a series of steps to take. Each step is taken within its own time. If you are focusing on accomplishing just this one step, doing your 100% best to get it done, you are spending less time living in a future which hasn't happened. You begin to see your future as the next moment in your life; you break away from trying to predict the end result of many layers of a major lifestyle change. What you experience in each of these moments will determine how you handle the next moment.

You begin to endure your journey. Faith begins to replace fear. We begin to have faith in ourselves, and our beliefs, and our ability to make it through. As a result, we start to battle less, which eliminates stress and anxiety from our lives. Our lives start to come into alignment and we begin to feel free. Once we believe that we have done everything we can in the best way we know how, the only action left to do is to leave it to God. We have no attachments to the past. There are no fears of the future. By going through a change in our lives, we may have to suffer a loss. But the loss is replaced with something else which often turns out to be better than we imagined. We start to enjoy what we have and count our blessings. We finally begin to realize that what we have and what we have experienced is exactly what we are supposed to live through. *This* is the essence of living life with *The Zing*.

If we are not ready to take a new direction, or we don't understand which direction to take, we can often become stuck at a Crossroad. We know a change needs to take place, but we are afraid of facing a new course. Even when we know which Crossroad to take, we still often choose the path of less resistance. But that same Crossroad that we avoid keeps coming back along our journey. It becomes a familiar Landmark. Often something dramatic happens in our life which makes us decide to change directions. As we begin to journey down that one road which will change our lives, we begin to realize that we can, indeed, live life with change. *The Zing* Highway is filled with all types of twists and turns and many Crossroads to choose from. So, embrace the power of change. It's up to you to decide which direction to take.

Learning how to live in the moment will help you deal with the Crossroads you encounter along *The Zing* Highway. Think back to a time in your life when you received either joyful or tragic news. These are the profound instances in your life where you can recall all of the details of a moment. Describe where you were, how you felt, why, etc.

_____

_____

_____

_____

_____

_____

_____

_____

_____

_____

_____

_____

_____

_____

_____

Do you remember standing at a Crossroad? Having to make the decision about which direction to take? Did you make the decision that was right for you?

_____

_____

_____

_____

_____

_____

_____

_____

_____

_____

_____

_____

_____

_____

_____

_____

_____

_____

The Tunnel

An avalanche of change begins with this drop of light.

6

The Tunnel

IN OUR TRAVELS, MOST OF US HAVE GONE THROUGH tunnels. They take us from one place to another by going through something that the road couldn't otherwise go around, like a mountain. Often these windy roads seem like they are leading us straight into the hills. It can be hard to see exactly where the road leads. As we travel on this highway, we begin to see a dark entrance into the mountains – a tunnel through to the other side. We know that once we go inside, daylight is left behind. We know we're in the middle when we look around and see only darkness. But just when we begin to think that the tunnel goes on forever, we begin to see a light ahead. It guides us back out into the daylight. The good news is that if it wasn't for the tunnel we would not have been able to get through the mountain to the other side.

How often have you felt like the problems in your life were like these mountains? Perhaps you have tried many times to find the path around. Or you may have even stopped traveling altogether. So, we need to find a Tunnel through. But because we can't see where it leads, and it looks dark inside, we become afraid of taking this particular Crossroad. However, your journey has led you exactly to this Landmark. Once through, you will be on your way to the most rewarding life you have ever imagined – *The Zing.*

Our journey towards the Tunnel starts when we reach a Crossroad in our lives knowing that something is not quite right. This feeling begins to haunt our lives and traps our thoughts, often sending us back to a moment of time — a past moment. It is the former moment in which we were happy for the last time. We go back to it and replay it in our mind because it allows us to feel good memories once again. These are the moments we use to provide a comparison to the things happening in our lives now. It can be any number of images or specific events. When we experience things that have a profound effect on us, they stick with us for better or worse. The question that must be asked of any moment in our lives is "Have you been able to put it in its place, learn from it, and move on"? As we have discovered, constantly revisiting the past means that we are not living in the moment. Looking back on our lives hoping it will bring back happiness is a sign that we may be looking to make *some* type of change. That type of change is what we experience in the Tunnel. Knowing and becoming aware that you may be avoiding a Tunnel is a Crossroad in itself.

It's like avoiding the dentist when you have a toothache. You don't really *want* to go. You've had the pain for a while and it always goes away. So you wait. Each time it comes back, it hurts more. You *know* that you should go and just take care of the tooth; but it's the fear of pain and discomfort that prevents you from going. You still avoid making an appointment. Then, the toothache comes back. But this time, the pain begins to outweigh the fear. You finally decide to go. It takes a few visits and several procedures along with perhaps more discomfort than you expected. But you know that it will eventually be finished. Thinking back to when it was just a dull ache, you realize that it might have been easier to have solved the problem sooner rather than wait until it got this bad.

Taking your first steps into the Tunnel can be just as frightening for all the same reasons as avoiding the dentist. Many know that a necessary change needs to take place in their lives but are too afraid of facing the unknown. For others, time is being spent pushing these problems back in their Dumpster, or wasting their Battery energy taking care of other people's problems. As you start to empty your Garage and take inventory, you begin to see some of the real issues in your life. By taking a good look at what's really been bothering you, you may decide that it is time to get rid of something that may have been holding you down for a long time. You begin to approach the entrance of the Tunnel and think about taking your first steps inside.

Most people enter the Tunnel in similar ways. It starts when you are unable to get over something in life, and represents the last moments of happiness you had before things changed. It can be a personal crisis, like the end of a relationship or a death of someone close to you. Or it can even be caused by something more from the outside, like the loss of a job or a home. In each case, you begin to pin your troubles on this one powerful life changing event. At first, you enter the Tunnel believing that these things are the root cause of all your troubles. When in reality, there may have been many other issues already at work in your life which caused you to become lost on your journey. But at this moment, the life that you once knew has changed and your path is now blocked. The only way to go is forward, into the Tunnel. We are able to face the fear of change ahead because there is change behind us as well.

At first, your journey into the Tunnel is filled with light because you can see where you are coming from.

You can keep your eye on something familiar. Many people will continue to do what feels comfortable even when they already know that it may no longer be right, or even healthy. An alcoholic or a smoker knows that their habit could kill them but they still drink and smoke. A drug addict knows that heroin is deadly, yet addicts will continue to poison themselves. A person critically overweight continues to make poor food choices. The contradiction in these two values can create paralyzing guilt which, in turn, stalls their journey. The same happens, on a less critical level, for someone at the beginning of their Tunnel who has experienced some type of loss. Visiting the grave of a loved one on a daily basis, going to restaurants that were favorites in a broken relationship, and keeping a newly married child's room "just the same" helps hold on to a former identity and former lifestyle. It is what's familiar; and its predictability brings comfort.

When you are doing activities that are familiar they shed light on your life and your path by providing you with pictures of who you are and where you have been. Eventually, you begin to remember the

Crossroad that you are on. You begin to acknowledge that something is different about the activity. You start to realize that you *aren't* that person anymore because one of the things that you used to measure who you were is gone. Eventually, those things that you think you want to do are not as satisfying as they once were. Once they have lost their appeal, you begin to do them less often. What is most important for you to realize is that you have, indeed, started to face change. You are going further into the Tunnel.

Time passes. We enjoy the things in our lives less and less. We become uncomfortable, fearful, and anxious because there is something happening which is taking the familiar things away. It is something which we find hard to understand, hard to come to terms with; it is something which is out of our control. This is when the journey begins to darken. As you approach the middle of the Tunnel, the walls start to shrink, the light begins to dim; it becomes almost impossible to move or see where you are going. This is when most people begin to lose hope, break down, and decide to go back and give up.

Relationships often travel in and out of the Tunnel several times. Married couples, in particular, can spend years building up anger and frustration inside before something happens to make them take a real serious look at their relationship. The real issues aren't the ones about toothpaste tubes and who doesn't pick up socks. But, often, this is what it becomes about in the beginning of the Tunnel. Talking about solving these "what bugs me about you" issues may often begin to provide a glimpse into hidden, inner problems that each partner has.

While in the Tunnel, couples are often faced with hard questions and uncomfortable answers. The journey often gets stopped when confronting these real issues because these are the problems that are not easily solved by creating new house rules. They fear the Crossroad; they fear the real change. So, they back out of the Tunnel. Many times, they believe that the work they have already done is all that they needed to do. They believe that the problem that brought them into the Tunnel in the first place has been solved. The relationship may feel more secure, but this false sense

of security is based only on the fact that the relationship is familiar. Better to return to what you know, rather than what is unknown. They return to what is familiar but this is *exactly* the problem. Even though a new set of relationship rules and guidelines may have been thoroughly worked out, there is still a lifetime worth of familiar old stuff in each Garage. This is the real root of most problems in relationships.

Once someone backs out of the Tunnel, they return being even more fearful than they were at the beginning of their journey because now they have begun to truly feel the pains of separation for the first time. When a person is in such a state, there is almost nothing anyone could say to change their mind. Their thoughts go from "I will do this" to "I should have done this." They hold onto the life that they know is wrong because they believe that they can go and fix, or control, the outcome. They feel that they can "get it back." They return, and try to live life again, but nothing happens. They are not aware that facing necessary change will bring happiness; it is not something that is lost from the outside which can go back and get fixed. Sadly, many end their journey just before it really begins.

Each time someone goes into the Tunnel, they tend to go a bit deeper. As they go further, it gets darker, and more upsetting. It is important to realize that within each trip, you begin to learn about how you are really feeling about the relationship. You wind up back in the Tunnel because you see that living life in the past, in a relationship that you have already said needs to change, has no future. You know it has no future because you cannot see it inside the Tunnel. So, you push in a little further each time. It is dark and depressing and at some point, you reach the middle.

Change, and the awareness that comes with it, cannot happen until we reach the *nadir*, or middle, of the Tunnel. It is where all that is unknown about our lives exists. It is the point at which our past has permanently changed and we cannot see into the future. For those at the nadir, living life is absolutely unbearable. When bad things happen, we get stuck on them as if they were played on a movie screen so big that it blocks out the sun. We are surrounded by dense blackness. All we can see is this one instance of happiness – the time we want to return to – and the sadness — the time from which we are unable to escape. Every day we wake up becomes a repetition of the last. We no longer do the things that gave us pleasure and no longer try to be happy because, until things change, happiness is out of reach.

It is the lowest of the low. What happens here? Terrible pain. Undeniable fear. Enormous doubt. You question who you are and why you feel the way you do. You must face the answers to these questions honestly. Accept that they are not the answers to all of life's problems but are instead part of the solution that leads to another series of problems. You may ask, "What would make *this* worth my time; why would I *want* to put myself through this?" Because it is from these experiences we get a new understanding of the world and ourselves; because from this journey we receive patience and love, and a whole new means of discovery. We begin to *understand* how to live life with *The Zing*.

Can you get from point A (unhappiness) to point C

(happiness) without point B (the Tunnel)? Unfortunately many of us cannot. Because we are either headstrong or vain, we ignore the present because it hurts; and like Pascal said, "we wander about in times that do not belong to us." We push the pain away because that is the easiest thing to do. But that is not change, that is denial; and it sends us on the direct track back to the beginning of the Tunnel. Change can only happen through facing that which makes us unhappy. And since we are talking about changing our lives, this involves confronting ourselves. Many strong people would much rather deal with a friend or even an angry person at a bar than look in the mirror for a while and try to be at peace with the person they see.

You have already gone through tremendous changes in your life if you are at the middle. You have already faced many fears, changed many values and beliefs. Why would you go back to a future which is rooted in the past — a future with *no* future? It is a lifestyle that you have worked to leave behind. From the middle to the beginning is the same distance as the middle to the end. It is at this point that, perhaps for the first time in your life, you only need one belief to move forward – faith. If you have faith, everything else will always come to you; and I do mean always. Trust me when I tell you that if you can get to the middle — if you've already gotten that far — stay the course. It is, after all, the middle. You are half-way home.

Now is when you begin to do the real life-changing work. That means reading, praying, and finding people to counsel and guide you. Try to understand what happened in your life and understanding why you feel the way you do. The work also involves coming to grips with the false boundaries you placed in your life. You become aware of what your life is lacking so you can fill it up with your own gifts and not with objects of the world or with someone else. The work is learning to love yourself and learning to live in love. If we lived in love and trusted in God then we would be able to get all the good things into our lives and leave the bad stuff behind. We could learn to live our lives and deal with those moments that set us back, no matter how hard they were or how often they came. Everything has a specific purpose. We would stop trying to control our life, and start experiencing what *The Zing* has to offer.

The unknown is almost always frightening. The good news is things are never what they appear to be. But it's always better than a past that we know all too well that we inhabit but, as Pascal said, do not actually live in. Once you get to the middle, know that just beyond it, a pinhole of light lingers in the distance. I promise, within that pinhole is the whole world; a future of your own, free from the disappointments and failures of yesterday. That pinhole of light will open up in front of you as if God pulled back a curtain and let the light pour into an old and dusty room. An avalanche of change begins with this drop of light. The walls of the Tunnel will open up and then fall away, and all around you is the promise of everything you wanted to do but couldn't imagine doing. I promise you that on the other side of the Tunnel, life will be better than you could have ever imagined.

Has the Tunnel become a familiar Landmark along your journey? Describe what you have experienced by looking at the Tunnel from the outside.

_____

_____

_____

_____

_____

_____

_____

_____

_____

_____

_____

_____

_____

_____

_____

_____

_____

If you have been inside a Tunnel along your journey, how far did you go in before you turned back? What prevented you from continuing forward? What tools can you take in with you on your next journey inside which could help you stay the course?

_____

_____

_____

_____

_____

_____

_____

_____

_____

_____

_____

_____

_____

_____

_____

The Beginning

I was able to go from living life to loving the life that I was living.

7

The Beginning

YOU MIGHT THINK THAT ONCE YOU ARE through the Tunnel, you will have reached the end. The truth is just the opposite. As you get to the other side, you begin to live life with *The Zing*. A life which is built upon awareness from within. A life which is lived from moment to moment with choices that are made based upon what is happening now. A life that knows change is good because it allows you to experience what's next.

There were times in my journey that I couldn't imagine looking forward to what was going to happen next. The future was filled with fear and the past was filled with regret. And I felt stuck in the middle. It was easy to blame life changing events as having caused my sadness. What was not so easy was admitting that the sadness existed long before everything else.

Becoming aware that the unhappiness came from within was a defining moment along my journey. If I can have sadness in my soul, then don't I also have the ability to replace it with happiness? By learning what made my life sad helped me to become aware of all the things packed away in my own Garage. I knew that before I could begin to take on a better way of living, I had to get rid of the old ways of thinking and old ways of feeling.

Identifying anger, resentment and disappointment wasn't too difficult. Having to work things out with people helped me to set up better boundaries. Slowly, I began to find out who I wanted to have in my life and which people were just draining my Battery. I decided to no longer allow their opinions and judgments to determine how I felt and what I believed. Making this choice brought me to another Crossroad — discovering why I allowed them to make me feel bad in the first place.

Knowing why I felt the way I did was where the real work began. At times, I felt like my life was coated with layers of dried up clay. Each time I discovered something, each time I came out of denial, it felt like a layer of clay broke away. Each time a layer broke off, I felt a bit lighter. I began to take a look back and see years of living with so much weight on my shoulders. All these things, stuffed away in my Dumpster, had begun to overflow into all parts of my life; and onto the important people in my life. It began to unconsciously drive my decisions because these old beliefs were dumped in there by someone or something else.

Seeing inside yourself, becoming aware of what you have been carrying around, is almost as scary as taking the steps to change it. This is often where many people stop their journey into the Tunnel. I believe that most people cannot make it through the Tunnel unless they have people to guide them. They are the Light Bulbs in your life – people that carry you along when your energy and will power are low. Amazingly, my relationship with two of these people, John and Beverly, started long before my journey and on a whole different level. When we first met, I never would have guessed that our relationships would have become what they are today. These are the types of relationships you have when you live life with *The Zing*.

Together with reading, prayer and counseling, I began to face the new choices in my life and the changes that go along with them. Taking a look back, if it were possible to take a snapshot of all the things I got rid of, it would have been an overwhelming sight. It was equally as overwhelming at the time when I was looking at the problems from the inside out. How to begin? I started by trying to live in the moment as often as possible. I gave myself permission to choose to do something "just for now." As time went on, many of the things that I was doing just for now became things that I did more frequently. I began to see that the changes I was slowly starting to make were pushing me forward. By making my own choices for my life, I began to learn what I wanted to keep, and what I really needed to eliminate.

What I needed to get rid of were all those things that I never truly accepted as my own but that had somehow found their way into my Garage. Parents, teachers, my religion and society had an important influence on my way of thinking. As I was beginning to question and explore the Crossroads of my life, I also began to question some of my basic beliefs. This is not to say that I abandoned what I had learned. By taking a complete inventory, I was able take each experience in my life and break it down into the good parts and the bad parts.

I found it difficult at times to come to terms with many of the experiences and events of my life. Hardest of all was learning how to see my son's death as something more than a senseless tragedy. How could the good possibly exist within something that was so profoundly bad? Looking back to when my mom died, I realized that all I did to cope with this loss was to stuff away my feelings. I didn't want to deal with the bad side of this loss so I just put it aside. However, putting it aside led me no where closer to living a better life. Now that I had already begun to make changes, I knew that I had to find a way to not only celebrate the good, but also co-exist with the bad.

It takes the one to know the other. Good cannot exist without knowing the opposite. The good is what is brought from moment to moment. It brings comfort and familiarity to think about joyful and fun events. Thinking about the good things in my life gave me renewed power to continue through the darkest parts of my Tunnel. But the bad was equally as powerful in my life. It pulled in the other direction. The emotions attached to it were as dark as the Tunnel itself. I could feel myself at another Crossroad. In order to go on, I knew I had to start letting these feeling out so I could begin to understand how to learn to live with them. Because it takes the one to know the other.

This was perhaps the most difficult part of my journey. I began seeing so many things within me that

I didn't know were there. It was like I was beginning to see behind a mask that I had been wearing for years. Grief, anger, resentment, frustration – I learned to recognize what each one felt like. I gave myself the permission to experience what they felt like. I became aware that each one existed within me.

Now I was truly able to begin emptying out my life. Each event, each experience could be dealt with on many levels because I was aware. I would look at each and put the negative things in what I like to call the Co-existing Box. It's almost like a reference library for the bad things in my life. When I'm in a situation where I feel that negative pull, I can go back into the Box and recognize the emotion before it sends me down the wrong path. Things in the Box are familiar because I have done the work to recognize and be aware of them. Knowing that I had already gone through the things in the Box, I became less fearful of the changes ahead. I found it easier and easier to choose to do the work. As the weight of my old life began to lift, I began to feel lighter. I made room in my Garage for those things that I truly wanted in there – those things that I worked hard to bring into my life, under my own power.

Profound loss brought about profound change. I started my journey looking for the answer to why Michael died. I got the answer. But I found it in places where I never would have looked. I had to experience the loss. I had to submit myself to the work. I had to endure my journey. My life permanently changed on July 22, 1998 and *that* was the lesson. Change happens and there is not much you can do to control it.

Change goes on all around, every day, each moment. Sometimes you can't see it and other times you can't escape it. I learned that the only thing to do is to let it happen. Fighting it wastes energy; denying it wastes time. When I decided to let go and flow through it, I felt more freedom than I ever had in my life. My past no longer controlled my present choices. Choices made "for now" had no ties to the future because the future could change. I live my life in the moment, doing the best I can, making the best decisions I can and leave the rest for God to handle. I was free to live without regret and worry. Looking back on all the difficulties that came through my life, I realized that I needed to experience these events in order to get to where I am today. I feel that God gave me these things to handle in order to help me learn about life. What I hadn't done, up until this point in my life, was listen.

Each moment in my life had a specific purpose for a specific reason and it was meant to be experienced at that time. The choices that I made in that moment were the only things I could control. The choices that I made then led me to the next moment. Dealing with each new moment was based upon living through the last moment. Each new moment brings new experiences into my life. Each new experience gives me the opportunity to experience more about life.

This is the very heart of living life with *The Zing*.

I was able to go from living life to loving the life that I was living. But this level of love and zest for living was much higher than I ever imagined. It goes far beyond the normal routines and the basic happiness. It's a level of life that knows change is always good, even when it brings difficulty. I live this life knowing that something new, fun, and exciting is what is always next. I wait for it with more passion in my heart and soul than anything else in my life.

I have discovered that *The Zing* Highway is endless. The more I travel its roads, the more people begin to travel along with me. Sometimes I help them; sometimes they help me. Each person travels their own path, but the destination is the same. I believe that Michael, and, through him, God, has brought people into my life at just the right time. You are part of my journey right now because you are supposed to be. It is hard to believe that what began as an incredible loss gave me the opportunity to discover an incredible new life. When you live your life with *The Zing*, you want to tell everybody that you have found some of life's best kept secrets. For me, I now have the opportunity to pay back what my son has given me by paying it forward to you.

Continue your journey!

We hope you enjoyed *The Zing*. If you would like to share your comments and stories, visit our website and sign in our Guestbook. We would love to hear from you.

Order books, merchandise, audio books, and more at our on-line store at www.ronvillano.com. Volume discounts available.

Join our mailing list to receive special announcements, up to date information about future events and promotions, and to find out when Ron will be in your area.

Embrace the Power of Change ™

K

Ron Villano, LLC
1650 Sycamore Avenue
Suite 39
Bohemia, NY 11716

631-758-8290

www.ronvillano.com

Embrace the Power of Change

Ron is available to speak at your:

- ℭ organization ℭ fundraising event

- ℭ college campus ℭ school ℭ group

- ℭ business ℭ community center

Bring *The Zing* to your area

Visit

www.ronvillano.com

for more information.

R

Ron Villano, LLC
1650 Sycamore Avenue
Suite 39
Bohemia, NY 11716

631-758-8290

NOTES

NOTES

About The Author

Ronald P. Villano, M.S., ASAC is a dynamic and inspirational speaker and highly successful leader in personal and professional counseling. His innovative techniques have brought inspiration together with the simplicity of learning how to embrace change as a part of life.

Ron's life dramatically changed when his youngest son, Michael, was killed in a car accident. Working through this deep and significant loss, Ron began to transform his life by walking the difficult path toward self-awareness. He spent several years searching for the answers that only came from within. His pursuit for this inner peace led him to intensely redefine and redirect his life. This profound spiritual and personal awareness is his guide for living life in a higher, more rewarding, and more passionate way.

Ron began to share *The Zing* in his life through counseling, book club groups, and seminars. His simple and easy to understand approach consistently empowers and motivates others to begin their own personal journeys.

Ron is the Director of Family and Personal Counseling and has a private practice in Psychotherapy in Bohemia, New York.